# NAPOLEON HILL'S

## THE LANGUAGE OF

# THOUGHT

# NAPOLEON HILL'S

## THE LANGUAGE OF

# THOUGHT

### LEVERAGE YOUR THOUGHTS TO ACHIEVE YOUR DESIRES

BY THE NAPOLEON HILL FOUNDATION

COMPILED BY JENNIFER JANECHEK, PHD

Published and Distributed by
SOUND WISDOM
PO Box 310
Shippensburg, PA 17257-0310
717-530-2122
info@soundwisdom.com
www.soundwisdom.com

Cover Design by Eileen Rockwell
Text design by Susan Ramundo

ISBN 13: 978-1-64095-242-3
ISBN 13 eBook: 978-1-64095-243-0

For Worldwide Distribution, Printed in the U.S.A.
4 5 6 / 26 25 24 23 22

# EDITOR'S PREFACE

Although all of Napoleon Hill's books, speeches, articles, and courses address the power of thought to translate our desires into physical reality, there is no single work that offers a simple formula for understanding, generating, and directing our thoughts to create the success we desire. Through my work with *Outwitting the Devil*—one of Hill's most popular books that illuminates the ways that our thoughts get poisoned by doubts, fears, and negative environmental influences—I uncovered a theory of thought language whose application holds incredible power to transform one's mindset, craft more powerful thoughts, build influence, and attract opportunities. This, I quickly realized, was perhaps the most powerful unexplored concept in Hill's success system. I set about studying Hill's entire oeuvre—from his earliest works to his more recent, yet-unpublished lectures—in order to isolate a straightforward, easy-to-implement process for learning and speaking the language of thought.

Yes, thought is a language that, like any other system of communication, must be learned and practiced in order to make effective use of it. It has its own syntax and grammar—in other words, there is a specific method for:

- creating thoughts out of impulses (like meaningful words from nonsensical sounds);
- arranging our thoughts in a structure that is comprehensible to the subconscious mind and to Infinite Intelligence (like syntax, or sentence structure); and

- magnetizing our thoughts to be more persuasive to the subconscious mind, other individuals, and Infinite Intelligence (like punctuation, figurative language, and other mechanisms for adding interpretive and meaning-making value to language)

If, as Hill suggests, our thoughts hold the power to transform our greatest desires into their material counterparts, then our efforts to achieve success can either be hindered or accelerated based on our understanding of and facility with the language of thought. By gaining fluency in this language, we can enlarge our capacity for achievement and enjoy the fruits of peace of mind and improved interpersonal relationships. Study and apply the formula contained in this book, compiled from extensive research into Hill's manuscripts and recordings, and you will maximize the ability of your thoughts to generate lasting change in the material world. Support your efforts through group study, for the context of a book club or Master Mind group can boost your ability to translate theory into practice—into *action*. Once you learn to speak the language of thought, you will be able to live out Hill's timeless dictum:

~~~

"Whatever the mind can conceive and believe
the mind can achieve."
—Napoleon Hill, *The Master-Key to Riches*

~~~

—Jennifer Janechek, PhD

# TABLE OF CONTENTS

# INTRODUCTION
## The Power of Your Thought

*There is something about the power of thought that seems to attract to a person the material equivalent of his aims and purposes. This power is not man-made. But it was made for man to use, and to enable him to control much of his earthly destiny.*

—Napoleon Hill, *Napoleon Hill's Greatest Speeches*

THE SINGLE MOST powerful tool available to human beings is not money, physical strength, influence, or a network; it is the mind. Our thoughts determine our outcomes in life, as well as our experience of the journey. As Napoleon Hill writes, "Thought is the only power that can systematically organize, accumulate, and assemble facts and materials according to a definite plan."[1] Whether we succeed in our personal and professional lives, and whether we are able to recognize and enjoy our success, is dependent upon the nature of our thoughts.

Thankfully, our thoughts are the sole element in our lives that are completely within our control. Regardless of external circumstances—no matter the environment into which we are born or in which we currently find ourselves—we can use our thoughts to translate our desires into reality. As Hill unreservedly states, "You can attract to you—nay…you *will* attract to you—the very things, or the very station in life, that you create in your thoughts."[2] In order to harness our thoughts to create material success, we do not require any personal advantage such as wealth, connections, or education. We simply need to leverage the mental resources already within our possession by cultivating a thorough understanding of the workings of the mind and the manner in which thoughts may be transformed into their physical counterparts.

The mind is the control station for our existence. It filters the infinite number of sensations that bombard our receptive organs; rearranges, combines, and stores a percentage of these impressions; and draws on memories and active thought impulses in order to guide our actions and reactions. All our mental and behavioral habits originate from the matter of thought. Thoughts are things—intangible, yet physical in nature. And because thought is matter—energy that signals to our bodies, our surroundings, and other bodies in proximity to us—it can be manipulated to create palpable results in the physical environment.

〰〰

"Man, alone, has the power to transform his
thoughts into physical reality; man, alone,
can dream and make his dreams come true."
–Napoleon Hill, *The Law of Success*

〰〰

Not only do our thoughts produce real effects in nature, but they also transform our character and personality. We come to resemble the nature of our dominating thoughts. Our personality will be magnetic, positive, and attractive if the mind is free of negative thoughts and emotions; our personality will be negative, alienating, and self-centered if our thoughts are characterized by fear and negativity. We are, therefore, the architects of our character and our life and must plan and assemble our thoughts as we would a house. But in order to do this, we first need to understand how thoughts work together as building units, and we need a blueprint to guide us toward arranging the units to fashion a solid mental framework. We need to acquire fluency in the language of thought.

As psychoanalysts found in the nineteenth century, the mind has its own language—a language that can be decoded to understand our subconscious fears and desires, yes, but also a language that can be restructured and enhanced to improve our mental and behavioral habits.

In order to get what we want in life, we have to learn to think more efficiently, more purposefully, and more programmatically. It is only when our thoughts are conditioned to be active, definite, and accurate that we can attract opportunities and riches into our life, as well as become more resilient to temporary defeat. Once we learn to govern the workings of our own mind, it becomes easy to build influence, garner support, and attract opportunities. As Rosa Lee Hill writes, "People actually pick up our thoughts, our state of mind, and reflect these thoughts right back to us in both attitude and spoken words."[3] There is nothing more powerful than a self-disciplined mind.

~~~

"We are the Masters of our Fate,
the Captains of our Souls, *because* we have
the power to control our thoughts."
—Napoleon Hill, *Think and Grow Rich*

~~~

This book provides a guide for generating more powerful thoughts so that you can live and work with more intention, joy, and success. When you learn to maximize your thoughts habits, you will attract the positive workings of Cosmic Habitforce, the universal law of nature that turns impulses into habits and habits into rhythms, which will give you increased momentum on your success journey. You will no longer be held back by fears, doubts, and difficulties, nor will the lures of procrastination and indecision thwart your progress. Everything will feel in sync and meaningful, like you are doing exactly what you are meant to be doing—and succeeding at it. Even when challenges come—and they will—you will thrive because you will see these not as setbacks but rather as opportunities in disguise. There are no limitations to the mind conditioned for success.

As you begin this book, realize that you are doing much more than reading a philosophy of the mind; you are starting a life-changing program of mental discipline. Too many success systems emphasize self-control as the key to individual achievement; however, self-control is merely the control over actions and words exhibited after already losing control of your mind. Mental discipline, in contrast, involves controlling your thoughts so that your actions and words are disposed for success. Mind control uproots negative thoughts and plants constructive impulses in their place, growing a fertile field of positive thoughts that seek outlet in definite plans of action. Gaining fluency in the language of the mind is the first step to disciplining your thoughts—the second is applying what you learn by speaking the language.

## LEARN THE LANGUAGE

1. What are your thought habits like? Consider memories, fears, thoughts, and desires that affect how you move through life.

Describe, as well, any patterns of thinking that impact your feelings, beliefs, and actions.

_____

_____

_____

_____

2. How are these thought habits serving, or not serving, you? How are they priming you for success and/or holding you back from realizing your full potential?

_____

_____

_____

_____

3. Imagine you are an architect, and you are building a house for yourself, except this time the house is your mind. How would you describe the ideal structure for your mind? How would its elements be characterized? What building materials would you use? What ones would you avoid? What would be the benefits of building the house in this way?

_____

_____

_____

_____

## CHAPTER ONE

# BEGIN WITH DESIRE

ALL THOUGHT IMPULSES originate from one of two sources: fear or desire. Both are emotions that are related to wanting, but they work in opposite directions. You desire what you DO want; you fear what you DON'T want. Because fear and desire are contrasting emotions, it is counterproductive to have both operating in your mind at the same time. They will vie for dominance until one succeeds at amplifying itself from an impulse of emotion to a full-fledged state of mind.

Fear is mental quicksand. The negative thoughts that originally gave fear a foothold enlarge and reproduce until the mind is completely paralyzed and unable to form constructive, positive thoughts. Indecision, procrastination, worry, greed—these are just some of the pernicious effects of operating from a position of fear. It is impossible to attain your chief aim in life if your thoughts are bogged down by fear. You will find yourself always moving backward, never forward; always missing opportunities, never recognizing or acting on them; always succumbing to failure, never seeing temporary defeat as an invitation to a newer, better plan.

The first step in controlling your thoughts, then, is to rid your mind of fear and its offspring: doubt, unbelief, greed, envy, jealousy, and superstition. You cannot productively focus on both the things you desire and the things you do not desire simultaneously. Autosuggestion, or the principle whereby our dominant, repeated thoughts seek outlet in physical form, does not discriminate between negative thoughts and positive ones. If there are strong fears present in your mind, your subconscious will work with the universe to translate them into material reality—just as it would constructive desires.

Begin now to change the chemistry of your brain by conditioning your mind to operate in a state of belief. In order to replace fear with faith, you must cultivate a positive mental attitude, for faith will reside only in a mind characterized by positivity. A positive mental attitude is like a fertile field in which you can plant the seeds of your definite major purpose. Cultivate this by focusing on how you can add value to others' lives. If you frame your desires in a context of service, they will be firmly embedded in a powerful emotional network that will repel fears, incite action, and invite the cooperation of Infinite Intelligence, the great storehouse of universal energy that some call "God" and others call "Nature." The formula below will help you cleanse your mind of lingering fears and complaints and begin anew with the seeds of faith.[1]

## FORMULA FOR FAITH

FIRST: I know that I have the ability to achieve what I want in life. I commit to performing the necessary actions, continuously and persistently, regardless of obstacles that come my way.

SECOND: I recognize that the dominating thoughts of my mind will reproduce themselves in outward action and eventually translate themselves into physical reality. Therefore, I will concentrate my thoughts daily on the type of person I wish to become—positive, benevolent, enthusiastic, decisive, prompt, and steadfast.

THIRD: Because of the principle of autosuggestion, I realize that any desire I persistently hold in my mind will eventually seek expression in material form, so I will dedicate time each day to feeding my mind thoughts of belief in my abilities, including the ease with which I can translate my desires into reality.

FOURTH: I recognize that desire, in and of itself, does not guarantee an individual success. Anyone can have a desire; what separates truly successful individuals from the rest of the population is their ability to evolve their desire into a consuming passion and their willingness to take action on it. With that in mind, I commit to using the principles outlined in this book to cultivate my thought impulses into definite thought habits and, eventually, rhythms of thinking that have greater force in attracting their aims. I will not dishonor my deepest desires by allowing them to remain in wish or hope form; I will render them active through their intentional development and implementation.

FIFTH: I fully realize that lasting success can never be built upon injustice or untruth, so I will refrain from engaging in any activity that threatens the rights or livelihood of others. I will seek to provide service to all mankind through my efforts to achieve success, and I will focus on inviting cooperation from others, rather than subduing or surpassing them.

Once you clear your mind of negativity and create a state of mind characterized by belief and self-confidence, you can identify the desire that will become your definite major purpose. No definite major purpose will have power unless it is backed by desire. For as Hill writes, "A definite chief aim would be meaningless unless based upon a deeply seated, strong desire for the object of the chief aim. Many people 'wish' for many things, but a wish is not the equivalent of a strong DESIRE, and therefore wishes are of little or no value unless they are crystallized into the more definite form of DESIRE."[2]

~~~

"DESIRE is the seed of all achievement, the starting place, back of which there is nothing, or at least there is nothing of which we have any knowledge."
–Napoleon Hill, *The Law of Success*

~~~

Dispense with any self-imposed limitations and consider now what is the one thing you want more than anything else in life. You have already emptied your mind of doubts and fears, so you are not allowing concerns about money, education, time, or anything else stand in your way of determining your primary desire. Use your imagination—don't hold back. Think in big terms, but choose something that is within the range of what can be expected of a man or woman with your capabilities, age, and intelligence. Questions to consider include the following: What is the pinnacle of success for you? If you could accomplish one thing in life, what would it be? Is it a relationship? A business? A position? An amount of money? A charitable act? "No one can select your dominating desire for you, but once you select it for yourself, it becomes your definite chief aim and occupies the spotlight of your mind until it is satisfied by transformation into reality, unless you permit it to be pushed aside by conflicting desires."[3]

Note that your dominating desire must not violate the rights of others, and it should be something that you truly want—because once you set the wheels of this success system in action, the principles will deliver you the object you have determined to create or acquire, regardless of whether it is good or pleasant to you. In order to plant in your mind the seed of a desire that is constructive, make the creed below the foundation of your code of ethics and the bedrock of all your efforts to succeed.[4]

## THE FOUNDATION OF DESIRE

I wish to be of service to my fellow men as I journey through life. To do this, I have adopted this creed as a guide to be followed in dealing with my fellow beings:

To train myself so that never, under any circumstances, will I find fault with any person, no matter how much I may disagree with him or how inferior his work may be, as long as I know he is sincerely trying to do his best.

To respect my country, my profession, and myself. To be honest and fair with my fellow men, as I expect them to be honest and fair with me. To be a loyal citizen of my country. To speak of it with praise, and act always as a worthy custodian of its good name. To be a person whose name carries weight wherever it goes.

To base my expectations of reward on a solid foundation of service rendered. To be willing to pay the price of success in honest effort. To look upon my work as an opportunity to be seized with joy and made the most of, and not as a painful drudgery to be reluctantly endured.

To remember that success lies within myself–in my own brain. To expect difficulties and to force my way through them.

To avoid procrastination in all its forms, and never, under any circumstances, put off until tomorrow any duty that should be performed today.

Finally, to take a good grip on the joys of life, so I may be courteous to men, faithful to friends and true to God.

Once you have named your primary desire, the next step is to work to develop it from a hazy wish to a strong impulse of thought to, eventually, a driving passion. For although desires begin as a flash of inspiration, they must be fertilized with belief and nurtured to become a dominating obsession that transcends everything else. Over time, a strong desire properly cultivated will become a fact—a certainty that your definite chief aim is already within your possession; you merely have to find a way to claim it.

A strong desire is one that you can experience as real. Use all of your senses to give your desire multi-dimensionality. The language of thought is not restricted to the symbols and sounds that make up our spoken and written language; it is based more on sensory impressions and concepts than anything else. So if you cannot find the right words to describe your primary desire fully, use other means: Draw it. Find its music. Determine its texture, taste, and sound. Use all the means at your disposal to create a detailed image, or clip, of your desire. "Paint a picture of what you want that is so definite and clear that none—particularly yourself—can mistake it."[5]

Continue to use your imagination to experience your primary desire in all its sensory richness on a daily basis. By holding it at the forefront of your mind, you will ensure that your actions align with your intentions. What is more, you will activate the Law of Attraction, a universal force that acts upon a constant, deeply seated, strong desire to attract its physical counterpart, or at least the means of securing it. This law stimulates your mind to recognize objects, people, and opportunities within your environment that have bearing on your dominating desire. For example, if you desire a particular position, suddenly you will take more notice of training opportunities that will qualify you for the role you seek. You will find yourself drawn to individuals who have some connection with the desired organization or field, enabling you to build your network and gain access to more opportunities related to your chief aim.

Desire is a magnetic force. When its elements are not guided by a strong magnetic field, like that of your mind, they will lose their alignment and become weakened. But when in the presence of a strong guiding force, the impulses that create desire regain their unified directionality and acquire strength.

Desire is also a form of energy. When it is stored and not put into action, it remains latent—as potential energy—unless it is transformed into negative emotions or thoughts or diminished through aimless thoughts and actions. But when activated, its kinetic energy causes transformations in the physical environment, creating or securing your chief aim.

Begin now to magnetize and energize your mind with intense desire. In the next chapter, we'll explore how to solidify your desire into a definite major purpose.

## LEARN THE LANGUAGE

1. What can you do this very week to feed your mind mental food that will contribute to the formation of a positive mental attitude? List any books, blogs, audio or video content, or activities that will enable you to replace fear with faith. Schedule time in your planner each day to receive inspiration and encouragement from these sources.

   _____

   _____

   _____

   _____

2. Use the space below to draw or describe your primary desire. In creating the representation of your chief desire, employ all five of the senses. What does it look like? What does it sound like? Smell like? Feel like? Taste like? Harness the power of your imagination to create a vivid depiction of your chief desire in all its multi-dimensionality.

   _____

   _____

   _____

   _____

3. Intensify your desire until it becomes an all-consuming passion by revisiting the above description or image on a daily basis, experiencing it in as much sensory vividness as possible.

Record below any new insights that you gain about your primary desire, including any opportunities or connections that become available to you through the Law of Attraction, as you magnetize and energize your desire on a daily basis.

_____

_____

_____

_____

## CHAPTER TWO

# REFINE YOUR THOUGHT IMPULSES

ONCE YOU HAVE intensified your desire, the next step is to crystallize it into a definite purpose. Hill analyzed over 35,000 people from all walks of life and discovered a startling fact: only two out of every one hundred individuals had definiteness of purpose. Unsurprisingly, these two were the ones who were succeeding, while the others had drifted into mediocrity. As Hill emphasizes, "Nobody ever achieved anything in this world worth achieving without definiteness of purpose."[1]

What distinguishes a definite major purpose from a desire? A desire is an impulse of energy and emotion that stimulates your mind to action and activates the Law of Attraction to begin sending opportunities and resources in your direction. A definite major purpose is a desire that has acquired concrete form and substance, has been located firmly in time, and has had a price tag attached to it. In other words, it is a commitment to put forth specific actions, according to definite plans, to add value in tangible ways, by an established deadline, so that an individual can attain a specific object or achievement to which they have laid claim. This commitment must be made in writing, for the act of writing it down signals to your subconscious mind that you have resolved to achieve your specific aim, and it recruits your subconscious mind to assist you in your efforts. As Hill explains, "We first create the objective toward which we are striving, through the imaginative faculty of the mind, then transfer an outline of this objective to paper by writing out a definite statement of it in the nature of a definite chief aim. By daily reference to this written statement, the idea or thing aimed for is taken up by the conscious mind and handed over to the subconscious mind, which, in turn, directs the energies of the body to transform the desire to material form."[2] Once you create your definite major purpose, you begin to operate in a state of mind conducive to achieving exactly what you desire.

It is helpful to think about a definite major purpose as being like a photograph. Those familiar with taking pictures know that there are three things needed for a good photograph: focus, proper timing, and light. If you do not attend to these three things, you will likely get a blurry picture, or at the very least, an unclear, unsatisfactory one. As Hill explains, "The subconscious mind is like the sensitive plate of a camera and when you put on that plate a wishy washy, indefinite picture of what you want, you may be sure you will get a blurred result."[3] For this reason, you must put on the plate of your mind a clear picture of exactly what you want, when you want it, and what you will give in return for it.

~~~

"Definiteness of purpose is the foundation
of all personal power."
—Napoleon Hill, *Outwitting the Devil*

~~~

Decide what your definite major purpose in life will be. Take your desire, in all its vivid imagery and sensory richness, and cement it into a written promise to yourself and the universe. Identify (1) the exact thing you want (e.g., a specific amount of money, a specific position, a particular type of thriving business, a specific flourishing relationship, etc.); (2) the exact service or object you will provide in exchange for your major purpose (remember, you cannot get something for nothing); and (3) the definite date by which you will attain your major purpose. It is crucial that you write this formula on a piece of paper or in a notebook, sign it, memorize it, and repeat it aloud at least three times a day, fully believing in your ability to achieve your major purpose.

On the same piece of paper, write a definite plan for attaining the object of your desire. Describe in detail exactly why you believe you will accomplish your purpose, the deadlines by which you will complete each phase or element of the plan, and what you intend to give in return for your progress. Be careful not to ask for something that is not beneficial to others, for nature, according to the Law of Compensation, will return payment to each individual according to what they have contributed. If you injure others in your pursuit of success, you will reap damages in return. Moreover, be wary of including abstract, or overly general, elements in your definite major purpose. For "if your aim in life is vague, your achievements will also be vague, and it might well be added, very meager."[4]

~~~

"Know what you want, when you want it, why you want it, and HOW you intend to get it."
–Napoleon Hill, *The Law of Success*

~~~

Hill knew the importance of definiteness from firsthand experience. In 1919, after the end of World War I, he decided to reexamine his written document outlining his definite chief aim, and where it read "I will earn ten thousand dollars in 1919," he crossed it out and wrote "one hundred thousand dollars." He had determined to publish and edit the *Golden Rule Magazine* and knew he needed at least that much money to do so. Immediately after editing the amount, a man came to his office from Texas and invited him to the Texas oil fields to see the men who were becoming overnight millionaires. As Hill's visit neared the end, the man offered to employ Hill for a year for one hundred thousand dollars—to be paid at the end of the one-year term. The contract specified that if Hill quit before the year was over, he would not get a dime. As you might have expected, despite Hill's high performance, the man was so demanding that Hill was forced to resign and returned to Chicago without one cent of his money.

From this experience, Hill learned that his definite chief aim for 1919 was not specific enough. He should have written "I will earn *and receive* one hundred thousand dollars during the year of 1919." By including those additional two words "and receive," he would have written the need for payment into his consciousness and contract. He would have then been able to take the contract to his lawyer to ensure that he was paid for his efforts.

### HOW TO APPLY DEFINITENESS OF PURPOSE

FIRST: Write out a clear statement of your major purpose, sign it, and memorize it. Make sure to include:

- The exact thing you want
- What exactly you will give in return for it

- The definite date by which you will attain it
- Why you have established this as your purpose

SECOND: Repeat it at least once a day in the form of a prayer or affirmation. Make sure that you are praying in a spirit of gratitude for what you already have, because begging and complaining do not invite the positive collaboration of Infinite Intelligence. When you are grateful for the riches already within your possession, more will be added unto you.

THIRD: Discipline your mind to be definite in everything you want. If you practice definiteness in the small things, then it will be easier to be definite about the large things.

FOURTH: Write out a clear definite outline of the plan or plans by which you intend to achieve the object of your purpose, and give each element of the plan a date by which it must be completed. For each stage of the plan, clearly define what you intend to give in exchange for your progress. Remember, you can never get something for nothing—and if you do, it won't stay with you for long.

By applying definiteness of purpose, you will condition your mind to complete the actions necessary to attain exactly what you want. This conditioning requires you to cultivate a deep and enduring capacity for belief. All prayer is answered within the mind, which is why you have to use language that your subconscious mind and Infinite Intelligence understand: the language of faith. Belief translates the written or spoken language you use to articulate your definite major purpose into the language of thought, a language of pure essences—where there is no gap between a word and the reality it represents. Condition your mind to generate thought in a state of definiteness and belief, and you will refine your thought impulses to become definite thoughts and, eventually, powerful thought habits.

~~~

"One's dominating desires can be crystallized into
their physical equivalents through definiteness of
purpose backed by definiteness of plans."

−Napoleon Hill, *Outwitting the Devil*

~~~

Definiteness is also the greatest protection you can offer your mind from the aimlessness that will derail you from accomplishing your major purpose. If you want to rise above the 98 percent who lack definiteness and can never find lasting success, you must take possession of your mind and control your thoughts so that you avoid procrastination, indefiniteness, and indecision. Establish for yourself a mental rule that you will produce only active, definite thoughts that are grounded in belief and directed toward your chief aim, and you will become more attuned to the opportunities that surround you. You will feel your intuition expanding, but what it really will be is your sixth sense—the creative imagination—becoming more receptive to the thought impulses in your environment that align with your definite major purpose. The sixth sense will help you process these thought impulses and use them to refine your definite plans for attaining your chief aim. You will discover that this process can be greatly aided—or diminished—by the nature of your emotions, which is why the next chapter turns to guidelines for controlling the emotions with which you energize your thoughts.

## LEARN THE LANGUAGE

1. Write a clear statement of your definite major purpose, sign it, and memorize it. Make sure to include:

- The exact thing you want
- What exactly you will give in return for it
- The definite date by which you will attain it
- Why you have established this as your purpose

_____

_____

_____

_____

Carry this statement with you, or place it in a prominent place in your home, and repeat it to yourself at least three times a day in a state of full faith in your ability to achieve it.

2. Write out a clear definite outline of the plan or plans by which you intend to achieve the object of your purpose, and give each element of the plan a date by which it must be completed. For each stage of the plan, clearly define what you intend to give in exchange for your progress.

_____

_____

_____

_____

3. Identify three areas of your life, or three activities, in which you need to be more definite (procrastinate less, be more decisive and engaged, and approach it with a clear sense of how it

connects with your definite major purpose). Make a plan for becoming more definite in these three areas.

_____

_____

_____

_____

## CHAPTER THREE

# CONTROL YOUR EMOTIONS

NOW THAT YOU have identified your definite major purpose and conditioned your mind to operate in a state conducive to its attainment, you must raise the frequency of your thought impulses so that they have more force and impact—on your subconscious mind, on Infinite Intelligence, and on other individuals. The way to stimulate your thought impulses to vibrate at a faster, more effective rate is to apply constructive emotions to them.

Your subconscious mind—what Hill occasionally terms your "inner audience"—is most influenced by emotionalized thought impulses. As Hill says regarding the subconscious mind, "You must speak its language, or it will not heed your call. It understands best the language of emotion or feeling."[1] He likens emotions "to yeast in a loaf of bread, because they constitute the ACTION element, which transforms thought impulses from the passive to the active state."[2] It is not until thought impulses have been activated by strong emotion that they will induce the subconscious mind to begin translating your desire into its material equivalent. Hill explains: "The subconscious mind is more susceptible to influence by impulses of thought mixed with 'feeling' or emotion, than by those originating solely in the reasoning portion of the mind. In fact, there is much evidence to support the theory, that ONLY emotionalized thoughts have any ACTION influence upon the subconscious mind."[3]

〜〜

**"The subconscious acts first on the dominating desires which have been mixed with emotional feeling."**
—Napoleon Hill, *Think and Grow Rich*

〜〜

Strong emotions not only recruit the subconscious mind to transmute one's desires into reality, but they also stimulate the creative imagination into action. Also known as the "sixth sense," the creative imagination is the faculty of the mind through which "hunches" and inspiration are received. When the conscious mind is vibrating at an exceedingly rapid rate, as through the presence of strong emotion, the creative imagination begins receiving thought impulses from the ether, both from Infinite Intelligence and from others' minds, and processes them to generate new plans for attaining your definite chief aim. Emotions, then, are responsible for opening a direct line of communication between finite man and the Infinite (universal intelligence), and they are a required ingredient for creativity, which is necessary to conceiving practical plans of action.

〜〜

**"The creative faculty of the mind is set into action entirely by emotions, and *not by cold reason*."**
—Napoleon Hill, *Think and Grow Rich*

〜〜

Because both the subconscious mind and the creative imagination are heavily influenced by thought impulses that are mixed with emotion, it is important to familiarize yourself with the more important ones and to learn to distinguish between constructive and destructive emotions. There are seven major positive emotions and seven major negative emotions. Unfortunately, we do not have to do any work to have negative emotions infiltrate our thought impulses—that occurs automatically, as passive thoughts are subject to contamination by negative emotions. The positive emotions, on the other hand, are not automatically injected into our thought impulses. They must be added to them intentionally through the principle of autosuggestion. First, let's review the major positive and negative emotions, and then we'll explore how to cultivate positive emotions and suppress negative ones.

## THE SEVEN MAJOR POSITIVE EMOTIONS

The emotion of DESIRE
The emotion of FAITH
The emotion of LOVE
The emotion of SEX
The emotion of ENTHUSIASM
The emotion of ROMANCE
The emotion of HOPE

### The Emotion of Desire

Desire is the primary motivating force behind your definite major purpose. It is the intense yearning for a specific aim, experienced in the mind in rich sensory detail. "Back of all achievement, back of all self-control, is that magic something called DESIRE!"[4] Since we already covered desire in detail in the first chapter, we will move on to the second major positive emotion.

### The Emotion of Faith

Faith is the belief in one's ability to attain a desired end. It is a requisite for success because it sets in motion actual forces by transforming the vibration of thought into a spiritual vibration. Once the subconscious mind translates the thought vibration into its spiritual equivalent, it can transmit the vibration to Infinite Intelligence, as through prayer. "Faith begins with Definiteness of Purpose functioning in a mind that has been prepared for it by the development of a Positive Mental Attitude. It attains its greatest scope of power by *physical action* directed toward the attainment of a definite purpose."[5] You can voluntarily cultivate the emotion of faith by repeatedly feeding your subconscious mind affirmations of belief, by expressing gratitude for the riches already in your possession, and by taking action on your definite chief aim.

〰〰

"Desire backed by faith knows no
such word as impossible."
–Napoleon Hill, *Think and Grow Rich*

〰〰

### The Emotion of Love

Love is a stabilizing emotion that renders any actions we might take constructive. When expressed in a healthy form—that is, not in a way that brings pain to the individual—it provides sanity, balance, and reason. As Hill suggests, "Love is the emotion which serves as a safety valve, and insures balance, poise, and constructive effort."[6] This emotion takes various forms: familial love, or love for parents or children; romantic love, or love for one's sweetheart; the love that exists in true friendship; and love for inanimate and nonhuman objects, such as nature. All shapes and shades of love can inspire reformation, or the desire to better oneself through the pursuit of one's definite chief aim. The emotion of love also provides a balancing function for the emotion of sex, combining with romance to form a mental trifecta that generates purpose, poise, and accuracy of judgment. Hill cautions, though, that love can also induce individuals to succumb to drifting, that state of aimlessness that leads to mediocrity and failure. For this reason, love must never be allowed to take over the mind in such a way that the individual neglects to develop definiteness.

### The Emotion of Sex

Faith and desire are psychical emotions that work on the subconscious mind in spiritual ways. The emotion of sex, on the other hand, is a biological force: it harnesses the body's physical drives to energize the mind's creative impulses. Hill identifies the emotion of sex as "the most powerful of all the stimuli which move people into ACTION."[7] However, it is also one of the most volatile emotions: its energy must be redirected from carnal ends and converted into other, more productive channels. In other words, you must take thoughts of physical sex expression and invest them in thoughts of a different, higher nature. When you channel sexual urges into thoughts pertaining to your definite major purpose, you acquire the following benefits: a super power for action, an irresistible force (personal magnetism or charisma) that draws others into your service, and unmatched creative powers. This latter capability is particularly important: anywhere creative genius is present, the transmuted emotion of sex must be present, for "the emotion of sex contains the secret of creative ability."[8]

### The Emotion of Enthusiasm

Like the emotion of sex, enthusiasm is an emotion that provokes the individual to action and stimulates the mind's creative faculties. It ensures that you will remain motivated in your pursuit of success, as it keeps your body and mind recharged and invested in your purpose and plans. This emotion is also contagious: it enables you to gain the cooperation of others in your endeavor— for who can remained unmoved by someone who is incredibly passionate about their goals AND is taking action on them? In addition, enthusiasm influences others to become more active agents in their own lives. This is because enthusiasm supports the principle of suggestion, whereby "your words and your acts and even your state of mind influence others."[9] With the aid of enthusiasm, your personality will become more dynamic, as your words and actions will be colored with invigorating energy, and you will develop the habit of concentration of endeavor. Those looking to cultivate the emotion of enthusiasm should engage in work or activities that provide them with the satisfaction of meaningful labor and service.

∾∾

**"ENTHUSIASM is a state of mind
that inspires and arouses one to put
action into the task at hand."**
—Napoleon Hill, *The Master-Key to Riches*

∾∾

### The Emotion of Romance

The emotion of romance collaborates with the emotions of sex and love to infuse your words and actions with calmness of purpose, amorous desire, and constructive effort. There should be an element of romance to all that we do. As with the emotion of sex, our romantic feelings can be channeled to other endeavors to generate excitement and interest. There is nothing sweeter than fresh romance: it energizes our movements, speeds up the vibrations of our thoughts, and develops keenness of focus on the object of our desire. Once we stimulate the mind with the emotion of romance, we can develop courage, willpower, and persistence that are unknown to us at other times.

## The Emotion of Hope

Hope keeps your focus fixed on the future—on the certainty that you will attain your definite chief aim. It is not to be confused with a hazy desire, a passive wish for fate to bring you what you seek. The constructive emotion of hope is a state of mind that is at peace because it is sure of future achievement. It is the largest contributor toward happiness, which "lies always in the future and never in the past."[10]

## THE SEVEN MAJOR NEGATIVE EMOTIONS

The emotion of FEAR
The emotion of JEALOUSY
The emotion of HATRED
The emotion of REVENGE
The emotion of GREED
The emotion of SUPERSTITION
The emotion of ANGER

In the great stream of life, there are two currents that flow in opposite directions. The side of the stream that carries an individual to success and fulfillment is made of positive emotions. The other side, which brings an individual to poverty, failure, and unhappiness, is comprised of negative emotions. It is the responsibility of every individual to learn to control their emotions so that their "chemistry of the mind" does not become toxic to them through the presence of harmful combinations of emotions. As Hill cautions, "The presence of any one or more of the destructive emotions in the human mind, through the chemistry of the mind, sets up a poison which may destroy one's sense of justice and fairness."[11]

～～

"The presence of a single negative thought in your conscious mind is sufficient to *destroy* all chances of constructive aid from your subconscious mind."
—Napoleon Hill, *Think and Grow Rich*

～～

Fear is the source from which all negative emotions flow. For this reason, it is helpful to catalog the six basic fears in order to discern which are influencing your thought impulses.

### The Fear of Poverty

The fear of poverty inspires poverty consciousness, leading to thought habits characterized by indifference, indecision, doubt, worry, and overcautiousness.

### The Fear of Criticism

The fear of criticism destroys one's creative faculties, one's freedom of thought, and one's initiative. The fear of criticism is particularly prominent in individuals whose parents were highly critical of them in childhood, causing them to develop an inferiority complex. It leads to thought habits characterized by self-consciousness, meek-ness, indecision, inferiority, extravagance, lack of initiative, and lack of ambition.

### The Fear of Ill Health

The fear of ill health is closely related to the fear of old age and the fear of death: all three come from humans fearing what happens after they die. It often produces the very symptoms it dreads because disease can begin as a negative thought impulse. It leads to thought habits characterized by an addiction to health fads, hypochondria, self-indulgence, and intemperance.

### The Fear of Loss of Love

The fear of loss of love arises when people worry about infidelity or abandonment by their romantic partner. It leads to thought habits characterized by jealousy, fault-finding, injudiciousness with money, and adultery.

### The Fear of Old Age

The fear of old age results from concern about the afterlife, poverty in old age, and loss of freedom of thought and activity resulting from the aging process. It leads to thought habits characterized by immaturity, nostalgia, inferiority, and a lack of imagination.

### The Fear of Death

The fear of death similarly results from concern about the afterlife. It leads to thoughts characterized by inaction, a fear of poverty, and religious fanaticism.

Search out the source of your negative emotions, determining which fear, or combination of fears, they are rooted in. Then use the faculty of willpower to discourage the presence of any negative emotion in your mind. The mind creates thought habits out of the dominating thoughts that are fed to it. Hill instructs: "Control of the mind, through the power of will, is not difficult. Control comes from persistence, and habit. The secret of control lies in understanding the process of transmutation. When any negative emotion presents itself in one's mind, it can be transmuted into a positive, or constructive emotion, by the simple procedure of changing one's thoughts."[12]

Develop an awareness of the emotions that are characterizing your thoughts. Actively cultivate positive emotions and transform negative emotions into positive ones. "Form the habit of applying and using the positive emotions! Eventually, they will dominate your mind so completely, that the negatives *cannot enter it.*"[13] Most people dissipate their emotions by sowing them in the wrong fields. Avoid this trap by investing your emotions in creating and carrying out plans to achieve your definite major purpose.

Beyond emotions, there are constructive mental stimuli that can temporarily, or even permanently, increase the rate of your vibrations of thought. These include music and the Master Mind alliance. Listening to music can stimulate your thought impulses to such a high frequency that your creative imagination becomes more alert, more receptive to vibrations from Infinite Intelligence and others' minds. Similarly, by forming and participating regularly in a Master Mind group, you can heighten your thought vibrations. In a Master Mind, the thought impulses of the different members, all directed toward the same aim, are jointly raised to a level unattainable by a single mind. Hill calls this psychic dimension of the Master Mind the "third mind": "No two minds ever come together without, thereby, creating a third, invisible, intangible force which may be likened to a third mind."[14] The spiritual units of energy generated from the Master Mind alliance allow the members to generate thought impulses that have more power over the subconscious mind and more magnetic force for attracting opportunities and answers.

Thought impulses that are characterized by desire and definiteness have power. Thought impulses that are backed by desire, refined by definiteness, and magnetized by a combination of the constructive emotions can create physical change in the world. When thought impulses attain a higher level of vibration through stimulation by the constructive emotions, they put an individual in direct connection with Infinite Intelligence, heighten the creative faculties, and influence others to offer their assistance. Remember: "The world is ruled, and the destiny of civilization is established, by the human emotions."[15] Learn to harness them for your success!

## LEARN THE LANGUAGE

1. For each of the positive emotions, identify a means for channeling it toward the pursuit of your definite major purpose. Note: The goal of this section is not to rationalize your desire by connecting it logically to the emotion in question; rather, you should conjure each one of these emotions by thinking of associated images and experiences and then transfer the emotion to your chief desire by holding your fixed desire and the emotion in your mind simultaneously. The result is not a motive structure for your desire (that's covered in the next chapter) but rather a more intense, more magnetic desire.

### The Emotion of Desire

*(What images and experiences create longing in your heart and mind? Conjure the feeling of intense yearning and apply this emotion to your chief desire. For this one, the emotion can equate to the thought impulse: You can think about and feel the intense longing that you have to achieve your definite major purpose. Magnify that longing by holding it in your mind alongside the thought of accomplishing your major purpose.)*

_____

_____

_____

_____

### The Emotion of Faith

*(What images and experiences [e.g., prayer, yoga, spiritual retreats] generate spiritual connection and/or supreme belief in yourself, a spiritual entity, or others? Conjure the feeling of complete trust and confidence resulting from connection with oneself, others, or a superior being and apply this emotion to your chief desire. For example, think about, or experience directly, the faith in oneself and the universe that results from practicing yoga; then transfer this calm, steady faith to your major purpose by holding this feeling in the same mental space as the thought of actualizing your chief desire.)*

_____

_____

_____

_____

### The Emotion of Love

*(What images and experiences create the feeling of deep affection that solidifies bonds between yourself and something outside of yourself? Consider all types of love—familial, romantic, friendship, love of nonhuman objects—and experiment with connecting the feelings of love generated by these different relationship types to your chief desire. For example, hold in your mind the feelings of deep affection for the natural world inspired by a beautiful sunset and apply these pleasurable feelings to your chief desire.)*

_____

_____

_____

_____

### The Emotion of Sex

*(What thoughts and experiences create sexual excitement, interest, and energy for you? Hold this emotion in your mind alongside the thought of accomplishing your major purpose, channeling the emotional energy toward it.)*

_____

_____

_____

_____

### The Emotion of Enthusiasm

*(What images and experiences get you excited and motivated to take action? Conjure the feeling of impassioned eagerness and*

*apply this emotion to your chief desire. Try thinking about what gets you the most excited about your major purpose; amplify your zeal for these aspects of your major purpose and then apply the enthusiasm to the thought of actualizing your chief desire.)*

_____

_____

_____

_____

### The Emotion of Romance

*(What images and experiences create romantic feelings for you? Romance can be the emotion that results from amorous interest, or it could be the interest and excitement you feel for an enjoyable experience—often a new one. Conjure the emotion of romance and apply it to your definite major purpose. For example, think about the romance of starting a new job you really wanted— the energy you bring to it, the excitement for all its mundane elements, the motivation to "go the extra mile"—and hold it in the same mental space as your definite major purpose.)*

_____

_____

_____

_____

### The Emotion of Hope

*(What images and experiences make you hopeful that a desire will come to fruition? Cultivate feelings of certainty that you will*

*accomplish your major purpose and stimulate the thought of your chief desire with the expectation that it will become reality.)*

_____

_____

_____

_____

2. Which negative emotion, or combination of negative emotions, is operating in your mind presently? Which of the six basic fears is responsible for each of your negative emotions? Locate the source, or sources, of each negative emotion in specific fears.

_____

_____

_____

_____

3. Make a plan for transforming your negative emotions into positive ones.

_____

_____

_____

_____

## CHAPTER FOUR

# FORMULATE YOUR COMPELLING MOTIVE STRUCTURE

**THOUGHTS REQUIRE BOTH** emotion and logic in order to entice the subconscious mind to translate your definite chief aim into material reality. Therefore, in addition to applying a mixture of the emotions detailed in the previous chapter, it is important to adopt a combination of compelling motives, or reasons for action, to place behind your definite major purpose. In other words, you need to embed your desire within a logical structure that gives it purpose and momentum—a momentum that will be attractive both to the subconscious mind and to the positive workings of Cosmic Habitforce, which solidifies behaviors into habits and habits into rhythms.

All voluntary physical action is inspired by one or more of the nine basic motives. "If you don't place back of your purpose a proper number of these motives you are not going to be invested in carrying out that major purpose after you adopt it."[1] You will not have a burning desire to initiate and complete actions toward achieving your definite purpose unless you have a motive that sets you on fire. The more of these motives you recruit for your aims, the more likely you will be to accomplish your goals.

Consider the catalog of the nine basic motives below, and determine which motive, or combination of motives, best serves your purposes by providing your desire with a solid logical framework in which it can gain strength. Note that the last two motives on the list are negative in nature, and although they can inspire action, it is usually toward a destructive end. It is best to ground your actions in positive motives; otherwise, you will undercut yourself by moving in the wrong direction or acting in ways that take value away from others, rather than adding it to them.

~~

"All individual achievement is the result
of a motive or combination of motives."
–Napoleon Hill, "Definiteness of Purpose"

~~

### The Desire for Love

The greatest of all motives is love—and not just physical attraction, but love in a broader sense. We feel love for our family, for our romantic partners, for our friends, for our country and communities. We feel love for both human and nonhuman creatures, animate and inanimate things. Love is the opposite of jealousy; it is rooted in contentment and gratitude. We love people and things because we appreciate their unique attributes and recognize the value that they add to our lives—and the value we bring to them as well. When we are motivated by our love for someone or something, it becomes incredibly easy to take the necessary steps to accomplish our aim because we see the value it will bring to our relationship. As Hill advises, "Let a man be motivated by Love and see how quickly this emotion is given wings for action through Faith.... The action becomes a labor of love."[2] Our actions become more purposeful because they are service oriented, and we reap more joy from our labors because we recognize that our efforts will strengthen our love.

### The Desire for Sex

This desire gives us the means of perpetuating every species on earth. When we are motivated by the desire to reproduce, we situate our actions and goals within a generational framework. Our behaviors gain increased significance because they are driven by a desire for legacy—for ensuring not only the continuation of the species and the family, the macro and the micro, but also the ability of posterity to enjoy the fruits of our labors. In addition to biological and generational considerations, the desire for sex is also anchored in the pleasure drive. As explored in chapter 3, by redirecting your desire for physical intercourse toward the accomplishment of your major purpose, you generate energy and incentive for achievement. And when you combine the motives of sex and love, you compound your motivation and gain enormous power for action.

### The Desire for Material Wealth or Money

This desire inspires us to develop our ingenuity and discover ways to build wealth. It is not rooted in a fear of poverty but rather in money consciousness—the awareness that we have all the tools we need at our disposal to increase our income and grow our net worth. When we are motivated by the desire for material wealth or money, our tendency to procrastinate diminishes, as it becomes easier not only to complete our responsibilities and tasks, but also to go the extra mile in our work. We seek out opportunities to expand our value and provide more service in our efforts to achieve our definite major purpose, rather than viewing each step along the way as a box that has to be checked off.

### The Desire for Self-Preservation

The desire for self-preservation is a relatively self-explanatory motivation. We all desire to live, and to live fully. Any time we can frame our desire in the context of its fulfillment of our basic human needs—food, shelter, clothing, belonging; the emotional and physical essentials for survival—we have a primal motivation to take action.

### The Desire for Freedom of Body and Mind

The majority of people desire wealth so that they can obtain freedom of body and mind. In general, human beings do not like to be beholden to other individuals. The more money we have, the more we are able to control our circumstances. When we direct our thoughts toward achieving freedom of body and mind and enjoying the satisfaction that comes from true self-sufficiency, we discover an almost spiritual urge to persist in our efforts. This motive is particularly compelling for individuals who are seeking to get out of debt, build wealth, start their own business, or gain independence in some other form.

~~~

"It is a well-known fact that men
will work harder for the attainment of an
ideal than they will for mere money."

—Napoleon Hill, *The Law of Success*

~~~

## The Desire for Self-Expression

As human beings, we tend not only to desire freedom of body and mind, but also the freedom to express ourselves—particularly in a way that enables us to gain public recognition. Hill describes this motive as the desire "to attract the attention of others and to impress them favorably."[3] When we believe our actions will result in the recognition of our special talents, gifts, and abilities, or will permit us to excel over others, we are less likely to experience burnout in our success journey.

## The Desire for Life after Death

The desire for life after death is the motive on which all religious activity is based. When our definite chief aim is rooted in a spiritual purpose or calling, we find the willpower to accomplish feats that would otherwise prove too difficult. Our weaknesses lose their power over us, as we gain the self-discipline and courage necessary to take consistent action on our goals. We believe ourselves to be supported by a higher being, so our efforts are magnified beyond our own abilities. Moreover, we believe our purpose to have eternal significance, which makes it that much easier to stay committed to achieving our definite chief aim.

### The Desire for Revenge

The desire for revenge is the first of two negative motives. When we are motivated by the desire to strike back—to take justice into our own hands and right a wrong that we believe we experienced—we might find the incentive to take action. However, the actions will surely send us in the wrong direction. The Law of Compensation dictates that our actions will be returned to us in kind, which means that any actions we take in a spirit of revenge will generate negative returns in our lives. Even if these negative consequences do not directly result from the actions we take in seeking revenge, they are certain to come at some point. As Hill writes, "Plans based on unjust or immoral motives may bring temporary success, but enduring success must take into consideration…Time."[4] It is therefore crucial that we assess our motivation to ensure it is free of the desire to get revenge on someone. Even if, for example, we desire success in order to rise above someone who has wronged us, we are sure to find ourselves on the negative side of hypnotic rhythm, the negative manifestation of Cosmic Habitforce that renders permanent destructive thought habits and behaviors and guarantees our ultimate failure.

### The Emotion of Fear

As with the desire for revenge, the emotion of fear inspires action that is undercut by destructive thought impulses. All six of the basic fears cause individuals to act, not in faith or service to others, but out of doubt, worry, and distrust. Such emotions debilitate the mind's reasoning faculty, preventing it from identifying productive means of accomplishing one's aims and encouraging it to take actions in the wrong direction. Fear, as a motive, will keep you in mental, emotional, spiritual, and financial poverty throughout your life, because it prevents you from using your personal initiative to create positive change in your life.

~~~

**"A strong motive forces one to surmount many difficulties."**
—Napoleon Hill, *Think and Grow Rich*

~~~

Place behind your definite major purpose one or more of these motives, and you will find the resistances of life fade into nothingness. Emotionalize your thought impulses, giving them strength and intensity, and then provide them with structure and direction by situating them within a compelling motive structure. When your thought impulses are directly linked to emotion and logic, you will discover the following benefits: Your mind will be prepared for action. Joy will crown your every effort. Self-discipline will become as natural as breathing. You will identify the secrets to influencing others, and you will strengthen your human relationships. For motives dictate not only the direction and ultimate success of our actions, but also the nature of our character.

## LEARN THE LANGUAGE

1. For each of the seven positive motives, identify a way of connecting it logically with your intentions in accomplishing your definite chief aim. In other words, how can you rationalize your purpose according to the logic of each of these seven constructive motives?

### The Desire for Love

*(How is your definite major purpose an expression of the love you feel for your family, your romantic partner, your friends, your community, or your country? For example, how are you helping someone or something you love, and in the process strengthening that relationship, by fulfilling your purpose?)*

_____

_____

_____

_____

### The Desire for Sex

*(For example, how is your definite major purpose driven by your desire to build a legacy? Or how is your definite major purpose a means of experiencing the pleasure of finding an outlet for your creative energy?)*

_____

_____

_____

_____

### The Desire for Material Wealth or Money

*(How will your definite major purpose bring you monetary rewards such as wealth, security, and independence either now or in the future? How does it provide material advantages?)*

_____

_____

_____

_____

### The Desire for Self-Preservation
*(How does accomplishing your definite major purpose enable you to ensure that you will have the basic physical and emotional necessities for survival: food, shelter, clothing, and belonging?)*

_____

_____

_____

_____

### The Desire for Freedom of Body and Mind
*(How does attaining your chief desire provide you with control over your circumstances? How does it enable you to dictate how your time, talent, and money are spent? For example, does it give you financial security and independence so that you are not beholden to your employer? Does it free you from some other form of emotional or physical bondage you are in?)*

_____

_____

_____

_____

### The Desire for Self-Expression
*(How does actualizing your chief desire enable you to express your unique individuality and obtain recognition for your talents?*

*What is impressive about it that is specific to your gifts, skills, and/ or creative pleasures?)*

---

---

---

---

### The Desire for Life after Death

*(How does accomplishing your major purpose build up treasures in the afterlife, thereby compounding its significance? Or how does it memorialize your identity on earth long after your death? For example, are you fulfilling a calling that has been placed upon you by a higher being? Are you providing a service to others that blesses their lives, and thus your own, in some way?)*

---

---

---

---

2. How is fear or the desire for revenge holding you back in your success journey? Do you find yourself beating against a wall, or moving in a backward direction, because you are motivated not by constructive impulses, but by negative ones?

---

---

_____

_____

3. Make a plan for eliminating any negative motives from your repertoire and replacing them with one or more of the seven positive motives.

_____

_____

_____

_____

## CHAPTER FIVE

# CREATE A THOUGHT HABIT THROUGH CONCENTRATION AND REPETITION

**AFTER STRENGTHENING YOUR** thought impulses by magnetizing them with constructive emotions, and after providing them with form and function through the adoption of a compelling motive structure, it is time to transform your thoughts into thought habits. A thought attains the level of habit through the forces of concentration and repetition. As habits increase in strength, they become a powerful rhythm. Hill explains, "Any impulse of thought the mind repeats over and over through habit forms an organized rhythm."[1] This organized rhythm makes it easier to generate new thoughts that align with your definite major purpose, and it attracts thought impulses and resources from external sources that will increase the ease with which you achieve your goals. Through the power of habit, our thoughts gain the force necessary to translate our desires into physical reality.

The principle that governs the process by which habits are fixed and rendered permanent is called Cosmic Habitforce. Being a principle of energy, it has two applications: positive and negative. The positive application, through which constructive habits are made permanent, is Cosmic Habitforce, whereas the negative application, through which destructive habits are made permanent, is called hypnotic rhythm. This universal law is the means by which nature maintains a perfect balance by creating a rhythm out of the repeated thoughts and behaviors of human beings. As thoughts become habits, they harmonize to form a structured pattern—a pattern that takes on its own nature. With Cosmic Habitforce, individual habits gain power through their networked relation to other habits that align with their purpose. In order to take advantage of this force, you must voluntarily put in your mind a thought that you want to keep (concentration) and continue bringing it back into your mind (repetition) until it is taken over by Cosmic Habitforce.

～～

"The person who thinks in terms of power, success, and opulence, sets up a rhythm which attracts these desirable possessions. The person who thinks in terms of misery, failure, defeat, discouragement, and poverty attracts these undesirable influences. This explains why both success and failure are the result of habit. Habit establishes one's rhythm of thought, and that rhythm attracts the object of one's dominating thoughts."
—Napoleon Hill, *Outwitting the Devil*

～～

Concentration, otherwise known as controlled attention, "is the act of focusing the mind upon a given desire until ways and means for its realization have been worked out and successfully put into operation."[2] Elsewhere Hill defines concentration as "the ability to think as you wish to think, the ability to control your thoughts and direct them to a definite end, and the ability to organize your knowledge into a plan of action that is sound and workable."[3] At its core, concentration is about possessing singularity of focus—both in your thoughts and your actions. We cannot do or think a dozen different things at a single time. Hill calls this person the "jack-of-all-trades"—someone who is trying to think and do too many things at once and accordingly lives a scattered, mediocre life. Rather than allowing our thoughts to be pulled in different directions, we must focus them on a singular aim. When we become skilled at holding definite thoughts in our mind, we activate the subconscious mind and the imagination to identify a practical plan for translating our desire into reality. This, in turn, makes it easier to create positive behavioral habits. It is nearly impossible to create long-term change in our actions without first changing the nature of our thoughts.

In order to transform your thoughts into thought habits, Hill recommends organizing "your thoughts by drawing a very clear and definite mental picture of the thing you wish to acquire or of the person you wish to be, and then concentrat[ing] on that picture until you transform it into a physical reality."[4] Blend together all the different subjects and ideas that create the perfect picture of your primary aim, and hold these thoughts in your mind until the subconscious mind solidifies them into habits, which attract the positive workings of Cosmic Habitforce.

～～

"Nothing great has ever been achieved without
the power of concentration."
–Napoleon Hill, *The Master-Key to Riches*

～～

The opposite of concentration is drifting, which occurs when individuals allow passive, negative, directionless thoughts to operate in their mind. These disorganized thoughts translate into habits of aimlessness and procrastination, which create a rhythm that ushers individuals toward failure. The mind wants to operate according to the path of least resistance, and the natural path of least resistance is fear and indecision. Whenever you are not intentionally placing constructive thoughts in your mind through concentration, your mind will begin to drift, and you will develop thought habits that work against your success. Eventually, hypnotic rhythm will take over and fix these directionless thoughts in a potent rhythm. Hill explains, "If the same thought is held in the mind, or left there by neglect, for a certain length of time, nature takes it over, through the rhythm of habit, and makes it permanent."[5] Once hypnotic rhythm has taken hold of your destructive thought habits, it becomes incredibly difficult to extricate yourself from the negative flow of energy. Therefore, it is crucial to foster constructive thoughts and dismantle negative impulses before they consolidate into a rhythm.

The corrective for drifting is definiteness and decisiveness. Ensure you are forming complete, purposeful thoughts out of which positive thought habits and behavioral habits can grow. Or as Hill says, "Be definite in everything you do and never leave unfinished thoughts in the mind. Form the habit of reaching definite decisions on all subjects!"[6] Acquire the habit of intentionally placing positive thoughts in your mind, and make sure to follow every thought to its logical end. Avoid hazy thoughts or ones that are not future oriented. Wishy-washy thoughts, as well as thoughts that are rooted in the past, are subject to the manipulations of negative external influences, causing your destructive thoughts to strengthen and multiply. You can avoid this trap through concentration, which enables you to cultivate concrete positive thoughts that will become habits of thinking.

A habit is formed through repetition. It creates a mental path whose grooves become deeper and wider as our thoughts and actions continue to travel over that same path. These grooves increase the ease with which we engage in the same thoughts and behaviors, and they make it difficult to think and act in different directions. Our habits grow out of our environment: "The human mind draws the material out of which thought is created from the surrounding environment, and habit crystallizes this thought into a permanent fixture and stores it away in the subconscious mind where it becomes a vital part of our personality, which silently influences our actions, forms our prejudices and our biases, and controls our opinions."[7]

～～

"Environment is the mental feeding ground out of which
the food that goes into our minds is extracted."
–Napoleon Hill, *The Law of Success*

～～

Because it is difficult for our mind to rise above our environment, we need to be attentive to the nature of our surroundings. Our thoughts will harmonize with our environment, so we must place ourselves in situations that are conducive to forming and maintaining constructive thought habits. For example, if you surround yourself with people who are poverty conscious, your mind will extract the fear and indecision from the thought impulses in your surroundings and create thought habits that will keep you in poverty. Similarly, if you place yourself in a context in which independence of thought, decisiveness, and self-discipline are valued and practiced, your thought habits will become characterized by definiteness and initiative. As we do the same things and think the same thoughts over and over again, our habits begin to resemble a cement block that cannot be broken. It is at this point that Cosmic Habitforce will take over and transform the habit into a permanent rhythm of thought or behavior.

If your thought habits are not currently supporting your success, you can form new mental pathways that attract the positive workings of Cosmic Habitforce. The best way to remove old habits that are not serving you is by creating new ones. As you form new habits, the old mental pathways will lose their sharpness and will begin to dissipate over time. Below is Hill's guide for forming desirable habits.[8] Once you replace destructive habits with constructive ones, you will no longer have to stand behind your desire and push it—"beyond this point, the desire will stand back of you and push you on to achievement."[9]

## HOW TO FORM A DESIRABLE HABIT

FIRST: At the beginning of the formation of a new habit, put force and enthusiasm into your expression. Remember that you are taking the first steps toward making the new mental path and that it is much harder at first than it will be afterwards. Make the path as clear and as deep as you can at the beginning, so that you can readily see it the next time you wish to follow it.

SECOND: Keep your attention firmly concentrated on the new path building, and keep your mind away from the old paths, lest you incline toward them. Forget all about the old paths, and concern yourself only with the new ones that you are building to order.

THIRD: Travel over your newly made paths as often as possible. Make opportunities for doing so, without waiting for them to arise through luck or chance. The oftener you go over the new paths, the sooner will they become well worn and easily traveled. Create plans for passing over these new habit-paths at the very start.

FOURTH: Be sure that you have mapped out the right path as your definite chief aim, and then go ahead without fear and without allowing yourself to doubt. "Place your hand upon the plow, and look not backward." Select your goal, then make good, deep, wide mental paths leading straight to it.

Our thoughts must acquire strength and consistency in order to fully harness the powers of the subconscious mind and Infinite Intelligence to translate them into reality. Like any language, the language of thought must be developed beyond concepts and words into complete sentences. The grammar and syntax of thought language are concentration and repetition, which enable us to fill out our thoughts so that they become a pattern—a pattern that Cosmic Habitforce reads and transforms into the story of our success. Are you ready to write your story with more powerful language?

**LEARN THE LANGUAGE**

1. How have your thoughts been characterized by indecision, aimlessness, and/or negativity? How have your thoughts been pulled in different directions so that your mental processes are bogged down by competing impulses?

_____

_____

_____

_____

2. How can you replace these thoughts characterized by drifting with more constructive thoughts? Make a plan for creating new thought habits that will attract the positive workings of Cosmic Habitforce.

_____

_____

_____

_____

3. Create a list below of thoughts and ideas that directly relate to your definite major purpose. Identify all the subjects that are necessary to paint a complete picture of its achievement.

_____

_____

_____

_____

4. Take a moment right now to concentrate upon your primary desire using the details identified in the last question. Fix in your mind a vision that blends together all of these elements, and then work to refine it by completing any details that are missing or hazy. Ensure this vision is oriented toward the future. While holding this vision in your conscious mind,

direct your subconscious mind to identify the best plan for actualizing your desire. Take notes below on the ideas that are generated through this exercise. Repeat this activity until a definite, practical plan becomes apparent to you.

_____

_____

_____

_____

CHAPTER SIX

# SAFEGUARD YOUR MIND WITH ACCURATE THINKING

UP TO THIS POINT, all of the strategies we have been describing are a form of offense: they are the means by which we can progress in our success journey by enhancing our use of thought language. But because the mind is subject to external influences, it is equally important that we bolster our lines of defense around our thoughts. The way to protect our subconscious mind from negative outside influences is through accurate thinking.

In order to safeguard our thoughts from destructive influences, we must engage in three mental processes:

➤ First, we must separate facts from mere information.
➤ Second, we must distinguish between important and unimportant facts—relevant and irrelevant ones.
➤ Third, we must become adept at organizing, classifying, and using the sound, relevant facts we retain in our minds.

To be sure that our thoughts are accurate, we must subject them to the control of the will and the faculty of reason. Hill writes, "Most so-called thinking is the work of the emotions without the guiding influence of self-discipline, without relationship to either the power of the will or the faculty of reason."[1] That is why the majority of thoughts produced are impotent at best and destructive at worst—they are undercut by the faulty logic that results from negative and uncontrolled emotions. Inaccurate thoughts result from ignorance, superstition, intolerance, and fear. Accurate thinking, in contrast, is characterized by freedom from dogma, bias, or the need for approval from others, and it is also infused with the emotions of faith, courage, hope, and definiteness of purpose.

〜〜

**"Accurate thinking is not possible without complete mastery of the emotions."**
–Napoleon Hill, *The Master-Key to Riches*

〜〜

Whenever the accurate thinker gathers information from external sources—or receives unsolicited information from others—he or she scrutinizes both the content of the message and the character of the source to determine its veracity. The accurate thinker puts aside all negative emotions and judges the message and its sender objectively. As Hill says, "The eyes of the accurate thinker sees facts—not the delusions of prejudice, hate and envy."[2] In contrast to the majority of people today, who prefer to remain in their own echo chambers so that their preconceived notions can be reinforced by everyone with whom they interact, the accurate thinker seeks out a multitude of perspectives and assesses each one with openness and controlled emotion.

The accurate thinker can quickly discern false or misleading information when it is tinged with slander or negative emotions. He or she does not accept without question public opinion, which tends to search out reasons for vilifying original thinkers. Rather than relying on the noise of the media or the whispers of gossip, the accurate thinker performs extensive research on information presented to him or her, consults with a Master Mind group, and leverages his or her own logical faculties to render an informed, impartial decision on a given matter. He or she allows no room for snap judgments—only scientific and accurate ones. As Hill describes this individual: "The accurate thinker has no opinions and makes no decisions which have not been submitted to, and passed upon by, the faculties of the will and the reason. He uses his emotions to *inspire the creation of ideas through his imagination*, but refines his ideas through his will and reason before their final acceptance. This is self-discipline of the highest order."[3] The accurate thinker maintains a firm standard of evaluation for all information and allows only facts to influence his or her thought processes.

Once the accurate thinker has distinguished facts from information, he or she must discern what constitutes an important and a relevant fact. According to Hill, "An important and relevant fact is any fact that you can use, without interfering with the rights of others, in the attainment of [your major] purpose. All other facts, as far as you are concerned, are superfluous and of minor importance at most."[4] More basically: "All thoughts that you can use in the attainment of your definite chief aim are important and relevant; all that you cannot use are unimportant and irrelevant."[5] One of the biggest differences between people who are successful and those who do not achieve their goals is the latter group muddles their thoughts with ideas that are not useful for attaining their definite major purpose. Concentration, as described in the previous chapter, will enable you to focus your thoughts on those ideas that align with your primary desire and filter out those that are irrelevant to your aims.

Finally, after separating fact from information and selecting only the most relevant facts to keep fixed in his or her mind, the accurate thinker becomes adept at organizing, classifying, and using the chosen thoughts. Engaging the faculty of the synthetic imagination, that portion of the mind that rearranges existing knowledge to produce new combinations, the accurate thinker orders and reorders facts until they generate a practical plan of action. In this way, accurate thinking goes beyond defense, participating in the mind's creative function as it "transform[s]...ideas into their most profitable, constructive form."[6]

~~~

"No one can be entirely free spiritually, mentally, physically, and economically without learning the art of accurate thinking."
—Napoleon Hill, *Outwitting the Devil*

~~~

The three mental processes described above are all a matter of controlling your thoughts, which is entirely within your power. Although these processes occur within the mind, there are two additional elements that can increase your ability to engage in accurate thinking. The first of these is your physical health. If you are not taking care of your body, it clouds your mind and prevents accurate thinking. In particular, it is important to consume healthy foods that support your cognitive processes. Foods that are too rich or that cause indigestion can slow down your reasoning faculty and generate negative emotions that obstruct rational thought.

The second external element that impacts your ability to think accurately is your relationships. If you are married, the quality of your thoughts can be raised or lowered depending on the nature of your partnership. As we explored in the previous chapter, our environment is the source from which the material of our thoughts is drawn. In a harmonious marital union, our minds can join together and generate higher-level thoughts. However, if our union is not harmonious, we are susceptible to inaccurate thinking and the habit of drifting. Our other relationships, such as our friendships and work relationships, can also influence our thoughts. But aside from our marriage relationship, the most impactful relationship on our thoughts is the one with our Master Mind alliance. When we participate in a harmonious group of likeminded individuals who encourage independent thinking and refuse to accept failure as final, we can take advantage of the "third mind" created from the alliance: the spiritual energy generated through the affinity produces a force that increases the frequency at which every member's thoughts vibrate, enhancing their creative and logical abilities.

Hill offers six principles whose comprehension is critical for accurate thinking.[7] Follow these guidelines for protecting your mind from negative external influences that inhibit accurate thinking. After all—"accurate thinking…is the solution to all men's problems, the answer to all his prayers, the source of opulence and all material possessions."[8]

## LEARN TO THINK ACCURATELY

**To learn how to THINK ACCURATELY…one must thoroughly understand:**

FIRST: That the mind can be controlled, guided, and directed to creative, constructive ends.

SECOND: That the mind can be directed to destructive ends and that it may, voluntarily, tear down and destroy unless it is with plan and deliberation controlled and directed constructively.

THIRD: That the mind has power over every cell of the body and can be made to cause every cell to do its intended work perfectly, or it may, through neglect or wrong direction, destroy the normal functionary purposes of any or all cells.

FOURTH: That all achievement of man is the result of thought, the part that his physical body plays being of secondary importance, and in many instances of no importance what-soever except as a housing place for the mind.

FIFTH: That the greatest of all achievements, whether in literature, art, finance, industry, commerce, transportation, religion, politics, or scientific discoveries, are usually the results of ideas conceived in one man's brain but ACTUALLY TRANSFORMED INTO REALITY BY OTHER MEN, through the combined use of their minds and bodies.

SIXTH: The majority of all thoughts conceived in the minds of men are not ACCURATE, being more in the nature of "opin-ions" or "snap-judgments."

Once you have mastered the art of accurate thinking, you will experience a freedom unknown to other individuals, the vast majority of whom allow the noise of the media and the naysayers to disrupt their thoughts and steal their peace of mind.

## LEARN THE LANGUAGE

1. Create guidelines below for distinguishing between facts and information. Use these guidelines as a standard to follow whenever you receive external ideas.

_____

_____

_____

_____

2. Create guidelines below for distinguishing between relevant and irrelevant facts. Use these guidelines as a standard to follow to when determining which facts to grant access to your subconscious mind.

_____

_____

_____

_____

3. Identify three steps you can take to improve your health in order to improve your ability to think accurately.

_____

_____

_____

_____

4. How can you leverage your relationships to improve the quality of your thoughts? If you are not part of a Master Mind group, make a plan for forming one so that you can take advantage of the psychic and cognitive benefits it provides.

_____

_____

_____

_____

# CONCLUSION
## Communicating in the Language of Success

*Spiritual and economic freedom, the two highest aims of which human beings are capable, are available only through the proper use of the mind.*
— Napoleon Hill, *Outwitting the Devil*

YOU NOW HAVE the tools you need to understand, create, and direct the language of thought. But comprehension is only half the journey; as with any language, you must apply what you learn by communicating in the language of thought to develop true fluency in it. The steps you take now to speak and interpret this language will determine the efficiency with which you achieve your definite chief aim. For the language of thought is the language of success: the subconscious mind and Infinite Intelligence, those two psychic forces that provide us with inspiration, refine our plans for achievement, and sustain us through the challenges that come our way, speak only in this language. Without the aid of these forces, the journey to translating your desires into reality will be significantly longer and more difficult.

Commit now to using the organ of your mind with more intentionality and intensity. Practice the principles outlined in this book with regularity and the support of a Master Mind alliance or study group, and your facility for the language of thought will develop such that you will enjoy more success in the pursuit of your chief aim and greater freedom in all areas of life.

1. Identify the burning desire whose attainment would be the pinnacle of success for you. Rid yourself of any fears that diminish the intensity of this desire, and replace these fears with faith in your ability to translate your desire into reality.

2. Refine your thought impulses related to your chief desire into a definite major purpose. Remember, a definite major purpose is *a commitment to put forth specific actions, according to definite plans, to add value in tangible ways, by an established deadline, so that an individual can attain a specific object or achievement to which they have laid claim.*

3. Magnetize your definite major purpose by emotionalizing your thought impulses with the positive emotions of desire, faith, love, sex, enthusiasm, romance, and hope.

4. Back your thought impulses with logic by packaging them in a compelling motive structure using one or more of the following constructive motives: the desire for love, the desire for sex, the desire for material wealth or money, the desire for freedom of body and mind, the desire for self-expression, and the desire for life after death.

5. Use concentration and repetition to transform your thoughts into mental habits that attract the positive workings of Cosmic Habitforce, the universal law of nature that turns habits into rhythms and gives you increased momentum on your success journey.

6. Protect your mind with accurate thinking, separating facts from mere information, distinguishing between important and unimportant facts, and effectively organizing, classifying, and using the sound, relevant facts you retain in your mind.

These six principles are the building blocks of the language of thought: desire, purpose, emotion, motive, concentration, repetition, and accuracy. They are the nonsensical sounds that, when arranged and combined in the proper way, form a comprehensible speech that compels your subconscious and Infinite Intelligence to work in your favor in translating your desire into material reality. As you will discover, this speech is far more powerful than any traditional human system of communication because it is not a language of mere words or signs; it is a language of impressions that directly correlate with their object, which means there is no chance of misinterpretation. Whatever you communicate using the language of thought will generate real and lasting effects in the physical world. There is no greater force for obtaining the results you desire.

Learn the language of thought—transform your potential for achievement!

## LEARN THE LANGUAGE

1. Based on your own understanding of the principles contained in this book, how would you describe thought as a language that can be learned and practiced?

_____

_____

_____

_____

2. Make a plan for revisiting these chapters to improve your mastery of the building blocks of language through individual or group study.

_____

_____

_____

_____

# NOTES

### INTRODUCTION

1. Napoleon Hill, *The Law of Success* (Shippensburg, PA: Sound Wisdom, 2021), 247.
2. Napoleon Hill, *Napoleon Hill's Greatest Speeches* (Shippensburg, PA: Sound Wisdom, 2017), 79.
3. Rosa Lee Hill and Napoleon Hill, *How to Attract Men and Money* (Shippensburg, PA: Sound Wisdom, 2021), 77.

### CHAPTER 1

1. This was adapted from Hill's self-confidence formula in *Think and Grow Rich* (Shippensburg, PA: Sound Wisdom, 2017), 74–75.
2. Hill, *Law of Success*, 176.
3. Ibid., 44.
4. Ibid., 126–27.
5. Hill, *Greatest Speeches*, 80.

### CHAPTER 2

1. Hill, *Greatest Speeches*, 195–96.
2. Hill, *Law of Success*, 176.
3. Napoleon Hill, *Napoleon Hill's Positive Influences*, The Napoleon Hill Foundation Archives, Wise, Virginia, United States, 44.
4. Hill, *Law of Success*, 44.

## CHAPTER 3

1. Hill, *Think and Grow Rich* (Shippensburg, PA: Sound Wisdom, 2017), 296.
2. Ibid.
3. Ibid., 295.
4. Hill, *Law of Success*, 126.
5. Hill, *The Master-Key to Riches* (Shippensburg, PA: Sound Wisdom, 2018), 166.
6. Hill, *Think and Grow Rich*, 283.
7. Ibid., 181.
8. Ibid., 262.
9. Hill, *Law of Success*, 104.
10. Ibid., 102.
11. Hill, *Think and Grow Rich*, 284.
12. Ibid., 284.
13. Ibid., 298.
14. Ibid., 251–52.
15. Ibid., 276.

## CHAPTER 4

1. Hill, *Napoleon Hill's Positive Influences*, 49.
2. Hill, *Master-Key*, 166.
3. Napoleon Hill, *Outwitting the Devil* (Shippensburg, PA: Sound Wisdom, 2020), 240.
4. Ibid., 197–98.

## CHAPTER 5

1. Hill, *Outwitting the Devil*, 159.
2. Hill, *Law of Success*, 182.

4. Hill, *Greatest Speeches*, 80.

5. Hill, *Outwitting the Devil*, 160.

6. Ibid., 155.

7. Hill, *Law of Success*, 182–83.

8. Ibid., 185.

9. Ibid., 178.

**CHAPTER 6**

1. Hill, *Master-Key*, 232.

2. Hill, *Law of Success*, 172.

3. Hill, *Master-Key*, 232.

4. Hill, *Law of Success*, 174.

5. Ibid., 168.

6. Ibid., 179.

7. Ibid., 175–76.

8. Hill, *Outwitting the Devil*, 238.

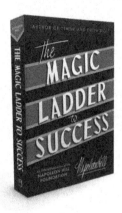

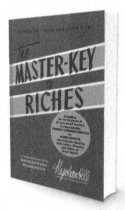